I0781425

Tupac Shakur: The Conscience of Hip Hop

Throughout the history of hip-hop music, few figures have been as iconic and influential as Tupac Shakur, whose lasting impact continues to be felt even today. Born in 1971 in East Harlem, New York City, Tupac was raised in a tumultuous environment marked by poverty, violence, and social upheaval. His mother, Afeni Shakur, was an active member of the Black Panther Party, and Tupac's early childhood was shaped by her political activism and the struggles of his community. At the age of 12, Tupac and his family moved to Baltimore, where he began to develop an interest in rap music and poetry. However, the move proved to be difficult for Tupac, and he soon found himself in trouble with the law.

In 1988, Tupac and his family moved to Oakland, California, where he became involved in the local rap scene. He joined the group Digital Underground as a backup dancer and rapper, and soon gained recognition for his powerful lyrics and raw delivery. In 1991, Tupac released his debut album, 2Pacalypse Now, which tackled issues such as police brutality, racism, and poverty.

The album was met with critical acclaim and controversy, with some critics accusing Tupac of promoting violence and misogyny. However, Tupac defended his music as a reflection of the harsh realities of life in the inner city.

Over the next few years, Tupac released a string of successful albums, including Strictly 4 My N.I.G.G.A.Z. (1993) and Me Against the World (1995). His music continued to address themes of social injustice and inequality, and he became known for his passionate and often confrontational style. However, Tupac's personal life was also marked by controversy and turmoil. He was involved in several altercations with other rappers, including a highly publicized feud with East Coast rapper The Notorious B.I.G. He also faced legal troubles, including a conviction for sexual assault in 1994.

Despite these challenges, Tupac's music and message continued to resonate with fans around the world. He was a vocal advocate for black empowerment and social justice, and he used his platform to raise awareness about issues affecting the black community. He was also known for his charismatic and complex persona, which combined vulnerability, anger, and a deep sense of purpose.

Tragically, Tupac's life was cut short when he was gunned down in Las Vegas in 1996. His death shocked the world and left a void in the music industry that has yet to be filled. However, his legacy has endured, and his influence can be seen in the work of countless artists who have followed in his footsteps. From Kendrick Lamar to J. Cole to Jay-Z, Tupac's impact on hip-hop music and culture remains as strong as ever.

In the years since his untimely death, Tupac Shakur's impact on hip-hop and popular culture has only grown stronger. His music, message, and persona continue to inspire artists and fans alike, and his influence can be seen in the work of countless performers across multiple genres.

One of the most notable aspects of Tupac's legacy is his commitment to social justice and political activism. Throughout his career, he used his music to address issues such as poverty, racism, police brutality, and inequality. He was a vocal advocate for black empowerment and spoke out against the systemic injustices that plagued his community. His willingness to take on controversial topics and speak truth to power has inspired countless artists to use their platform to effect change.

Tupac's influence can also be seen in the way he fused different genres and styles in his music. He was a skilled rapper, but he also drew on elements of R&B, funk, and rock to create a sound that was uniquely his own. His ability to blend different genres and create a diverse range of sounds paved the way for other artists to experiment with new sounds and styles.

In addition to his musical impact, Tupac's legacy is also defined by his complex and often contradictory persona. He was known for his tough exterior and aggressive lyrics, but he was also a deeply introspective and vulnerable artist. He wrote candidly about his struggles with poverty, violence, and addiction, and his willingness to show his emotional side helped to humanize him in the eyes of his fans. His ability to navigate these seemingly opposing forces - toughness and vulnerability, anger and empathy - has influenced a generation of artists who seek to express the full range of human experience in their music.

Perhaps one of the most enduring aspects of Tupac's legacy is his impact on popular culture beyond music. He was a gifted actor and appeared in several films, including Juice (1992) and Poetic Justice (1993).

His magnetic presence and natural charisma made him a natural fit for the screen, and his performances helped to broaden his appeal beyond the world of music.

Tupac's influence can also be seen in fashion, art, and literature. His signature bandanas, tattoos, and bulletproof vests have become iconic symbols of hip-hop culture, and his bold, unapologetic style continues to inspire fashion designers and trendsetters around the world. In addition, his poetry and writing have been published posthumously, and his influence can be seen in the work of contemporary poets and authors who seek to explore themes of identity, race, and social justice in their writing.

His music, poetry, and interviews were filled with thought-provoking and inspiring quotes that continue to resonate with people today. From his reflections on love, family, and social justice to his musings on life, death, and the human condition, Tupac's words offer a window into his soul and the issues that mattered most to him. Let us take a look at his most essential quotes through which we can gain a deeper understanding of his artistry, his passion, and his impact on the world.

Let me say for the record, I am not a gangster and never have been. I'm not the thief who grabs your purse. I'm not the guy who jacks your car. I'm not down with people who steal and hurt others. I'm just a brother who fights back. I'm not some violent closet psycho. I've got a job. I'm an artist.

First, I wanna say 'peace' to my mother. She's not here but I gotta give a 'peace out' to her because I wouldn't be here if it wasn't for my mother.

My mother taught me three things: respect, knowledge, search for knowledge. It's an eternal journey.

If we really are
saying rap is an art
form, then we got to be
more responsible for
our lyrics. If you see
everybody dying
because of what you
saying, it don't matter
that you didn't make
them die, it just
matters that you
didn't save them.

If you let a person
talk long enough
you'll hear their true
intentions. Listen
twice, speak once.

No matter what these
people say about me,
my music does not
glorify any image, my
music is spiritual if
you listen to it. It's
all about emotion,
it's all about life.

Please wake me
when I'm free
I cannot bear
captivity
4 I would rather be
stricken blind
Than 2 live without
expression of mind

I gotta big mouth, I can't help it, I talk from my heart, I'm real you know what I'm sayin whatever comes comes. But my controverse problems, It's not my fault, I try to find my way in the world you know, I try to be somebody instead of just, make money off of everybody. You know what im saying, so I go down paths that haven't been traveled before and I usually mess up, but I learn, you know what I'm saying, I come back stronger, I'm not talking ignorant, you know what I'm saying. So obviously put thought into what I do. So I think my mouth, my controverse, I have not been out of the paper since I joined Digital Underground, I've been in all, you know what I'm saying, my name has not been not uttered, you know what I'm saying, and that's good for me because I don't wanna be forgotten. If I'm forgotten then that means I'm comfortable and that means I think everything is okay.

I want to grow.
I want to be better.
You Grow. We all grow.
We're made to grow.
You either evolve
or you disappear.

I'd love to go back to
when we played as
kids, but things
change. And that's
the way it is.

Did you hear about
the rose that grew
from a crack in the
concrete? Proving
nature's laws wrong,
it learned to walk
without having feet.
Funny it seems,
but by keeping its
dreams it learned
to breathe fresh air.
Long live the rose
that grew from
concrete when no one
else even cared.

Keep ya head up.
Do what you gotta do.
And then, inside of you,
I will be reborn.

Instead of war on poverty, they got a war on drugs so the police can bother me.

Take ones adversity
Learn from their
misfortune
Learn from their pain
Believe in something
Believe in yourself
Turn adversity
into ambition
Now blossom
into wealth.

A woman bought you
into this world, so
you have no right
to disrespect one.

I'm 23 years old.
I might just be
my mother's child,
but in all reality,
I'm everybody's child.
Nobody raised me;
I was raised in this
society.

Every day, I'm standing outside trying to sing my way in: We are hungry, please let us in. We are hungry, please let us in. After about a week that song is gonna change to: We hungry, we need some food. After two, three weeks, it's like: Give me the food Or I'm breaking down the door. After a year you're just like: I'm picking the lock. Coming through the door blasting.

The seed must
grow regardless
Of the fact that
it's planted
in stone.

I'm known as a survivor now, I hope so, for the jail thing, bullets and everything, controversies and everything, I hope so. And I want to be in the future known as somebody. You know I want people to be talking about me like you know: "remember when he was real bad, remember when Tupac was real bad". You know what I mean, they do that about a lot of actors now, like John Travolta I read stories like "remember you were wild". And all these other people, and now they're like sweet hearts. We all should get that chance, I just want my chance.

The American Dream
wasn't meant for me
'Cause lady liberty's a
hypocrite, she lied to me
Promised me freedom,
education, equality
Never gave me nothing
but slavery
And now look at how
dangerous you made me
Calling me a mad man
'cause I'm strong and
bold.

My mama always used
to tell me: 'If you
can't find somethin'
to live for, you best
find somethin' to
die for.'

There's no way that Michael Jackson or whoever Jackson should have a million thousand droople billion dollars and then there's people starving. There's no way! There's no way that these people should own planes and there people don't have houses. Apartments. Shacks. Drawers. Pants! I know you're rich. I know you got 40 billion dollars, but can you just keep it to one house? You only need ONE house. And if you only got two kids, can you just keep it to two rooms? I mean why have 52 rooms and you know there's somebody with no room?! It just don't make sense to me. It don't.

And now I'm like a
major threat, 'Cause
I remind you of the
things you were
made to forget.

I am society's child.
This is how they made
me and now I'm sayin'
what's on my mind and
they don't want that.
This is what you made
me, America.

Where There is a will
there is a will
to search and discover
a better day

Where a positive heart
is all you need
to rise beyond
and succeed

Where young minds grow
and respect each other
based on their deeds
and not their color

when times are dim
say as I say
"Where there's a will
there's a way!"

That which does not
kill me can only make
me stronger
That's for real
And I don't see why
everybody feel
as though
That they gotta tell me
how to live my life
You know?
Let me live, baby,
let me live

We wouldn't ask why a
rose that grew from the
concrete for having
damaged petals, in turn,
we would all celebrate
its tenacity, we would
all love its will to
reach the sun, well, we
are the roses, this is
the concrete and these
are my damaged petals,
don't ask me why, thank
god, and ask me how

The trick is to never lose hope!

We talk a lot about Malcolm X and Martin Luther King JR, but it's time to be like them, as strong as them. They were mortal men like us and everyone of us can be like them. I don't want to be a role model. I just want to be someone who says, this is who I am, this is what I do. I say what's on my mind.

I'm not perfect. But
I'll always be real.

Currency means
nothing if you still
ain't free. Money
breeds jealousy.
Take the game from me;
I hope for better days.
Trouble comes
naturally. Running
from authorities. 'Til
they capture me, and my
aim is to spread more
smiles than tears.
Utilize lessons
learned from my
childhood years.

Here's a message to the new borns, waiting to breathe: if you believe then you can achieve. Just look at me, against all odds 'though life is hard, we carry on, livin' in the projects, broke with no lights on. To all the seeds that follow me- protect your essence, born with less, but you still precious.

God come save the
youth, Ain't nothin
else to do but have
faith in you, Dear
Lord I live the life
of a Thug, hope you
understand Forgive
me for my mistakes,
I gotta play my hand.

If God wanted me to be quiet he would've never showed me what he does.

Out of anger comes
controversy, out of
controversy comes
conversation, out
of conversation
comes action.

You have to work from one point to go to another. So I admire work ethic, I think it should be re-inforced through out our neigbourhoods, that everybody should work hard, practice makes perfect, you have to be diligent with what you want, you have to apply your self, you have to motivate your self. You have to do for-self by your self, and then you can do things for other people. But that's what I had to do, I had to do for-self.

Listen to the words
people say in their
lyrics, and tell me, if
that's some real shit,
if that's real to you,
you know what I mean.
Listen to what they
sayin', don't just bob
your head to the beat,
peep the game, and
listen to what Im
saying. Hold us
accountable for it.

I believe that
everything that you do
bad comes back to you.
So everything that I
do that's bad, I'm going
to suffer from it. But
in my mind, I believe
what I'm doing is
right. So I feel like
I'm going to heaven.

When your hero falls from grace,
all fairy tales are uncovered
Myth exposed and pain
magnified, the grace
pays uncovered
He told me to be strong,
but I confused to see it so weak
You say never to give up, and it
hurts to see what comes to be
When your hero falls soley the
stars, and so does the reception
of tomorrow
Without my hero, theres only me
alone, to deal with my sorrow
Your heart ceases to work, and
your soul is not happy at all
What are you expected to do,
when your only hero falls

Everybody's at
war with
different
things...I'm at
war with my own
heart sometimes.

This so called
'Home of the Brave'
why isn't anybody
Backing us up!
When they c these
crooked ass Redneck cops
constantly Jacking us up

What of a love unspoken?
Is it weaker without a name?
Does this love deserve 2 exist
without a title
because I dare not share
its name
Does that make me
cruel and cold
2 deny the world
of my salvation
because I chose 2 let it grow
people tend 2 choke
that which they do not
understand
Why shouldn't I be weary
and withhold this love
from MAN
What of a love unspoken
no one ever knows
But this is a love that lasts
and in secrecy it grows

Heaven ain't hard
to find; all you
gotta do is look.

Why am I fighting to
live, if I'm just
living to fight?
Why am I trying to
see, when there ain't
nothing in sight?
Why am I trying to
give, when no one
gives me a try?
Why am I dying to
live, if I'm just
living to die?

We are being wiped off
the face of this earth
At an extremely
alarming rate
And even more alarming
is the fact
That we are not
fighting back.

Cry later, but for
now, let's enjoy
the laughter.

If there be pain,
reach out 4 a
helping hand
and I shall hold u
wherever I am
Every breath I breathe
will be into u
4 without u here
my joy is through
my life was lived
through falling rain
so call on me
if there be pain

You never know how
strong you can be
until being strong
is the only choice
you have left.

When I say ' thug' I mean
not a criminal, someone
who beats you over the
head, I mean the
underdog. You could
have two people- one
person has everything
he needs to succeed and
one person has nothing.
If the person who has
nothing succeeds, he's a
thug. Cuz he overcame
all the obstacles.

It's like if you plant
something in the
concrete and if it
grow and the rose
petal got all kinds of
scratches and marks,
you ain't gonna say,
'Damn, look at all the
scratches and marks
on the rose that grew
from the concrete.'
You're gonna be like,
'Damn, a rose grew
from the concrete?'

You gotta find a
way to survive
cause they win
when your soul
dies.

There should be a class on drugs. There should be a class on sex education-a real sex education class-not just pictures and diaphragms and 'un-logical' terms and things like that.....there should be a class on scams, there should be a class on religious cults, there should be a class on police brutality, there should be a class on apartheid, there should be a class on racism in America, there should be a class on why people are hungry, but there are not, there are classes on gym, physical education, let's learn volleyball.

You can spend minutes,
hours, days, weeks,
or even months over-
analyzing a situation;
trying to put the
pieces together,
justifying what
could've, would've
happened... or you can
just leave the pieces
on the floor and move
the f*ck on.

It's time we stop
worrying, and get
angry you know? But
not angry and pick up
a gun, but angry and
open our minds.

Trust me
I never lose.
Either I win
or learn from it.

I don't see myself
being special; I just
see myself having more
responsibilities than
the next man. People
look to me to do things
for them, to have
answers.

America is the
biggest gang
in the world.

I know it seems hard
sometimes but
remember one thing.
Through every dark
night, there's a bright
day after that. So no
matter how hard it
get, stick your chest
out, keep ya head up.....
and handle it.

Be grateful
for blessings,
Don't ever change,
keep your essence.
The power is in the
people and politics
we address.

If I upset you, don't
stress. Never forget
That God isn't
finished with me yet.
I feel His hand
on my brain...
When I write rhymes,
I go blind and let the
Lord do His thang.

I'm not saying I'm going to rule the world, I'm going to change the world. But I guarantee I will spark the brain that will change the world. And that's our job. It's to spark somebody else watching us. We might not be the one, but let's not be selfish. And because we['re] not going to change the world, not talk about how we should change it. I don't know how to change it. But I know if I keep talking about how dirty it is out here, somebody's going to clean it up!

Marlon Brando is not a gangster-actor, he's an actor. Axl Rose and them are not gangster rock-and-rollers, they're rock-and-rollers right. So I'm a rapper, this is what I do. I'm an artist.

Celebrate life
through the music
through the spoken word
through the splatter of
colour on paper
or wood
or iron
or canvas
But celebrate your life
Celebrate your ability
to feel joy and sadness
Celebrate your
ability to feel!
Only then will we be
free to feel

The realest
people don't have
a lot of friends.

It's the game of life.
Do I win or do I lose?
One day they're gonna
shut the game down.
I gotta have as much
fun and go around the
board as many times
as I can before it's my
turn to leave.

Behind every sweet smile, there is a bitter sadness that no one can ever see and feel.

Strength is overcome
by weakness
Joy is overcome
by Pain
The night is overcome
by Brightness
and Love-it remains
the same.

Sometimes when I'm alone
I Cry,
Cause I am on my own.
The tears I cry are bitter and warm.
They flow with life
but take no form
I Cry because my heart is torn.
I find it difficult to carry on.
If I had an ear to confide in,
I would cry among my treasured
friend,
but who do you know
that stops that long,
to help another carry on.
The world moves fast
and it would rather pass by.
Then to stop and see
what makes one cry,
so painful and sad.
And sometimes...
I Cry
and no one cares about why.

My music is not for everyone. It's only for the strong-willed, the [street] soldiers music. It's not like party music- I mean, you could gig to it, but it's spiritual. My music is spiritual. It's like Negro spirituals, except for the fact that I'm not saying 'We shall Overcome.' I'm saying that we are overcome.

As long as some suffer
The River Flows Forever
As long as there is pain
The River Flows Forever
As strong as a smile can be
The River will Flow
Forever

I have no
patience for
anybody who
doubts me,
none at all.

But tomorrow I see a change, a chance to build anew, built on Spirit, intent of heart, and ideas based on truth. Tomorrow I wake with second wind and strong ideas of pride. I know I fought with all my heart to keep the dream alive.

I feel that what was
done in the dark will
come to light. There
are secrets everybody's
gonna find out about.

I believe honestly that
I can talk. I believe
that I have the ability
to reason, I have logic,
I have compassion,
I have understanding.
If we talk there's no
problem you know what
I'm saying. But that's
not what happened.
People used what they
heard in media and
that's how they come at
me, and then you know
we got a clash.

Never surrender, it's
all about the faith
you got: don't ever
stop, just push it
'till you hit the top
and if you drop, at
least you know you
gave your all to be
true to you, that way
you can never fall.

In USA, a black man only have like five years we can exhibit maximum strength, and that's right now while you a teenager, while you still strong, while you still wanna lift weights, while you still wanna shoot back. 'Cause once you turn 30, it's like they take the heart and soul out of a man, out of a black man, in this country. And you don't wanna fight no more.

Don't believe
everything you hear:
Real eyes, Realize,
Real lies.

I exist in the depths
of solitude pondering
my true goal Trying 2
find peace of mind and
still preserve my soul

A lot of people, black,
white, mexican, young
or old, fat or skinny
have a problem being
true to they self. They
have a problem looking
in the mirror and
looking directly into
their own souls. Only
reason I am who I am
today is because I can
look directly into my
face and find my soul

There's gon' be some
stuff you gon' see
that's gon' make it
hard to smile in the
future. But through
whatever you see,
through all the rain
and the pain, you
gotta keep your sense
of humor. You gotta be
able to smile through
all this bullshit.
Remember that.

You can't disrespect
the love. You can't
disrespect the
peace treaty.

We don't need no more rappers, we don't need no more basketball players, no more football players. We need more thinkers. We need more scientists. We need more managers. We need more mathematicians. We need more teachers. We need more people who care; you know what I'm saying? We need more women, mothers, fathers, we need more of that, we don't need any more entertainers.

Life's a test,
mistakes are lessons,
but the gift of life
is knowing that you
have made a
difference.

God, When I was alone,
and had nothing,
I asked for a friend to
help me bear the pain,
No one came, except God,
When I needed a breath
to rise, from my sleep,
No one could help me..
except God, When all I
saw was sadness, and I
needed answers, No one
heard me, except God, So
when I'm asked.. who I
give my unconditional
love to? I look for no
other name, except God.

I am a hard person to
love but when I love,
I love really hard.

Don't change on me.
Don't extort me unless
you intend to do it
forever.

I set goals, take
control, drink out my
own bottle, I make
mistakes but learn
from every one, And
when it's said and done,
I bet this brother be a
better one, If I upset
you don't stress, Never
forget, that God isn't
finished with me yet.

Fear is stronger than
love, remember that.
Fear is stronger than
love, all that love I
gave didn't mean
nothing when
it came to fear.

Death is not the
greatest loss in life.
The greatest loss is
what dies inside
while still alive.
Never surrender.

You know it's funny,
when it rains it pours
they got money for wars,
but can't feed the poor.

June 16, 1971 – Mama
gave birth to a hell
raisin' heavenly son.

If you're not dark
inside and you come
to this world, it'll
turn you dark... and
if you really have
Sunshine inside you,
it's not good to play
in the dark. It's just
gonna extinguish
your fire.

Measure a man by his
actions fully, from
the beginning to the
end. Don't take a piece
out of my life or a
song out of my music
and say this is what
I'm about, because you
know better than that.

The only thing that
can kill me is death,
that's the only thing
that can ever stop me,
is death, and even
then my music will
live forever.

NOTE TO THE READER:
In the next few pages let us look at
Tupac Shakur's studio albums
(not including posthumous releases)

2Pacalypse Now (1991)

"2Pacalypse Now" is the debut studio album by American rapper Tupac Shakur, released in 1991. The album is widely considered to be a politically charged and socially conscious work of art, tackling a wide range of social issues affecting young black people in America at the time.

The album opens with the track "Young Black Male," a powerful statement on police brutality and racial profiling, which sets the tone for the rest of the album. Shakur's lyrics address the pervasive racism and prejudice faced by young black males in America, painting a bleak picture of a society in which young black men are unfairly targeted by law enforcement and often left with few options for survival.

One of the most powerful tracks on the album is "Trapped," which tells the story of a young man who turns to drug dealing as a means of survival in a poverty-stricken neighborhood. The song paints a vivid picture of the harsh realities of life for many young black people in America, highlighting the economic and social forces that often drive them into lives of crime and violence.

Another notable track on the album is "Brenda's Got a Baby," which addresses the issue of teenage pregnancy and its impact on young mothers. The song tells the story of a young girl who becomes pregnant and is forced to raise her child alone, with little support from her family or community. The song is a poignant commentary on the challenges faced by young mothers in low-income communities, and the societal forces that often leave them feeling isolated and alone.

Throughout "2Pacalypse Now," Shakur's lyrics are raw, honest, and deeply personal, reflecting his own experiences growing up in poverty and struggling to make a life for himself in a society that often seems stacked against him. The album is a powerful testament to the resilience and strength of young black people in America, who continue to fight against injustice and inequality to this day.

Despite its critical acclaim, "2Pacalypse Now" was also controversial at the time of its release, with some critics and activists accusing Shakur of promoting violence and misogyny in his lyrics. However, many others saw the album as an important work of social commentary, shedding light on the issues faced by young black people in America and calling for change in a society that often seems indifferent to their struggles.

Overall, "2Pacalypse Now" remains an important album in the history of hip-hop, and is considered to be a classic example of socially conscious rap music. Its themes of social justice, economic inequality, and racial prejudice continue to resonate with audiences today, making it a timeless work of art that remains relevant and powerful more than thirty years after its initial release.

Strictly 4 My N.I.G.G.A.Z... (1993)

"Strictly 4 My N.I.G.G.A.Z..." is the second studio album by American rapper Tupac Shakur, released in 1993. The album is widely considered to be one of Tupac's most important works, showcasing his skills as a lyricist and social commentator while also cementing his status as a rising star in the world of hip-hop.

The album opens with the track "Holler If Ya Hear Me," a powerful statement on the struggles faced by young black people in America.

Shakur's lyrics address issues such as police brutality, poverty, and racism, painting a vivid picture of the harsh realities of life for many young black people in the United States.

Another standout track on the album is "I Get Around," a catchy and upbeat song that showcases Tupac's more playful side. The song features a sample from the Zapp & Roger hit "Computer Love" and was a commercial success, reaching the top 20 on the Billboard Hot 100 chart.

Tupac's lyrics are gritty and intimate, expressing his own firsthand encounters and the challenges he faced while trying to establish a meaningful existence. In tracks such as "Last Wordz" and "Words of Wisdom," Tupac addresses issues such as economic inequality and the failings of the educational system, calling for change in a society that often seems indifferent to the struggles faced by young black people.

Perhaps the most powerful track on the album is "Keep Ya Head Up," a heartfelt and uplifting song that celebrates the strength and resilience of black women in the face of adversity. The song is widely considered to be one of Tupac's most important works and has become an anthem of sorts for young black women around the world.

"Strictly 4 My N.I.G.G.A.Z..." is a deeply personal and socially conscious album that addresses a wide range of issues affecting young black people in America. Tupac's lyrics are powerful and insightful, and his talent as a storyteller and social commentator shines through in every track. The album is widely considered to be a classic example of socially conscious rap music and remains an important part of Tupac's enduring legacy in the world of hip-hop.

Thug Life: Volume 1 (1994)

"Thug Life: Volume 1" is the only studio album by the group Thug Life, which was formed by Tupac Shakur and several of his friends in 1994. The album is widely regarded as a classic in the genre of gangsta rap and features some of Tupac's most powerful and emotional lyrics.

The album opens with the track "Bury Me a G," which features a sample from the classic soul song "Never Can Say Goodbye" and sets the tone for the rest of the album. The song features Tupac rapping about his own mortality and the harsh realities of life as a young black man in America.

Another standout track on the album is "Cradle to the Grave," which features a haunting piano melody and lyrics that reflect Tupac's struggles with poverty and crime. The song is a powerful reminder of the toll that life on the streets can take on young people, and is widely regarded as one of Tupac's most emotional and personal works.

Tupac and his collaborators explore themes such as police brutality, gang violence, and the struggles faced by young people growing up in poverty. The lyrics are raw and unflinching, reflecting the harsh realities of life for many young people in America's inner cities.

One of the most memorable tracks on the album is "Pour Out a Little Liquor," which features a sample from the classic soul song "Walk on By" and is a tribute to Tupac's fallen comrades. The song is a heartfelt and emotional reminder of the toll that violence and crime can take on communities, and is widely regarded as one of Tupac's most powerful works.

"Thug Life: Volume 1" is a strikingly intimate and potent work, demonstrating Tupac's exceptional skills as a songwriter and narrator. The album's themes of struggle, survival, and redemption resonate with many young people around the world, and continue to inspire new generations of fans. Although Thug Life only released one album before disbanding, their influence on the world of hip-hop and popular culture remains strong, and the legacy of Tupac Shakur continues to be felt today.

Me Against the World (1995)

"Me Against the World" is the third studio album by Tupac Shakur, released in 1995 while he was serving a prison sentence. The album is widely regarded as one of Tupac's best works, and features some of his most personal and emotional lyrics.

The album opens with the track "Intro," which features Tupac speaking about his struggles with fame and his desire to make music that reflects his experiences as a young black man in America. The song sets the tone for the rest of the album, which explores themes such as poverty, crime, and the struggles of life on the streets.

One of the standout tracks on the album is "Dear Mama," a heartfelt tribute to Tupac's mother Afeni Shakur. The song features Tupac rapping about his mother's struggles and sacrifices, and the love and support she gave him throughout his life. The song became one of Tupac's most popular and enduring works, and is widely regarded as a classic in the genre of hip-hop.

Another memorable track on the album is "So Many Tears," which features a haunting piano melody and lyrics that reflect Tupac's struggles with depression and the trauma of his experiences on the streets.

The song is a powerful reminder of the toll that poverty and violence can take on young people, and is widely regarded as one of Tupac's most personal and introspective works.

One of the most emotional tracks on the album is "Can U Get Away," which features a sample from the classic soul song "Do Me, Baby" and is a powerful ballad about love and redemption. The song is a reminder that even in the midst of pain and struggle, there is always hope for a better tomorrow.

"Me Against the World" is a highly introspective and impactful work that highlights Tupac's exceptional abilities as a wordsmith and storyteller. The album's themes of struggle, survival, and redemption resonate with many young people around the world, and continue to inspire new generations of fans. Despite the challenges that Tupac faced during his life, his music and message continue to be celebrated and remembered today as a powerful voice for social justice and equality.

All Eyez on Me (1996)

"All Eyez on Me" is the fourth studio album by Tupac Shakur, released in 1996 on Death Row Records. The album is widely regarded as one of Tupac's greatest works, and features some of his most iconic and memorable tracks.

The album opens with the track "Ambitionz Az a Ridah," a hard-hitting gangsta rap anthem that sets the tone for the rest of the album. The song features Tupac rapping about his life on the streets, his struggles with the law, and his determination to succeed despite the odds.

Another standout track on the album is "2 of Amerikaz Most Wanted," a collaboration with Snoop Dogg that has become a classic in the genre of hip-hop. The song features Tupac and Snoop rapping about their experiences on the streets, their struggles with the police, and their determination to overcome the obstacles in their way.

One of the most memorable tracks on the album is "California Love," a collaboration with Dr. Dre that features a catchy hook and an infectious beat. The song became one of Tupac's biggest hits, and is widely regarded as a classic in the genre of hip-hop.

Another notable track on the album is "Life Goes On," a poignant ballad about loss and the struggle to move on in the face of tragedy. The song features Tupac reflecting on the deaths of his friends and loved ones, and finding solace in the memories they left behind.

Despite its many successes, "All Eyez on Me" also courted controversy due to its explicit lyrics and graphic depictions of violence. Some critics accused Tupac of promoting a culture of violence and misogyny, while others praised him for speaking truthfully about the harsh realities of life on the streets.

Tragically, Tupac was murdered just months after the release of "All Eyez on Me," and the album has since become a powerful symbol of his legacy and influence on the genre of hip-hop. Despite his untimely death, Tupac's music continues to inspire new generations of fans and artists, and his message of resilience, strength, and social justice remains as relevant today as it was during his lifetime.

The Don Killuminati: The 7 Day Theory (1996, released under the name Makaveli)

"The Don Killuminati: The 7 Day Theory" is the fifth and final studio album by Tupac Shakur, released posthumously in 1996 under the name Makaveli. The album was recorded in just seven days, and has since become a legendary work in the genre of hip-hop.

The album opens with the track "Bomb First (My Second Reply)," which features a hard-hitting beat and an aggressive flow from Tupac. The song sees Tupac firing back at his enemies and critics, and declaring his intention to take on all comers.

Another standout track on the album is "Hail Mary," a haunting and atmospheric song that features a memorable chorus and some of Tupac's most intense and emotional lyrics. The song is widely regarded as one of the greatest hip-hop tracks of all time, and has become a staple of Tupac's legacy.

One of the most notable tracks on the album is "Against All Odds," which features Tupac taking aim at his former friend and collaborator, The Notorious B.I.G. The song features some of Tupac's most scathing and confrontational lyrics, and is widely regarded as a classic diss track in the genre of hip-hop.

Tragically, Tupac was murdered just weeks before the release of "The Don Killuminati: The 7 Day Theory," and the album has since become a powerful symbol of his legacy and influence on the genre of hip-hop. Despite this untimely death, Tupac's music continues to inspire new generations of fans and artists, and his message of resilience, strength, and social justice remains as relevant today as it was during his lifetime.

www.ingramcontent.com/pod-product-compliance
Lightning Source LLC
Chambersburg PA
CBHW012258240726
48656CB00007B/2440